Name	Wishes and Comments

Name	Wishes and Comments

Name	Wishes and Comments

Name	Wishes and Comments

Name	Wishes and Comments

Name	Wishes and Comments

Name	Wishes and Comments

Name	Wishes and Comments

Name	Wishes and Comments

Name	Wishes and Comments

Name	Wishes and Comments

Name	Wishes and Comments

Name	Wishes and Comments

Name	Wishes and Comments

Name	Wishes and Comments

Name	Wishes and Comments

Name	Wishes and Comments

Name	Wishes and Comments

Name	Wishes and Comments

Name	Wishes and Comments

Name	Wishes and Comments

Name	Wishes and Comments

Name	Wishes and Comments

Name	Wishes and Comments

Name	Wishes and Comments

Name	Wishes and Comments

Name	Wishes and Comments

Name	Wishes and Comments

Name	Wishes and Comments

Name	Wishes and Comments

Name	Wishes and Comments

Name	Wishes and Comments

Name	Wishes and Comments

Name	Wishes and Comments

Name	Wishes and Comments

Name	Wishes and Comments

Name · Wishes and Comments

Name · Wishes and Comments

Name · Wishes and Comments

Name · Wishes and Comments

Name	Wishes and Comments

Name	Wishes and Comments

Name	Wishes and Comments

Name	Wishes and Comments

Name	Wishes and Comments

Name	Wishes and Comments

Name	Wishes and Comments

Name	Wishes and Comments

Name	Wishes and Comments

Name	Wishes and Comments

Name	Wishes and Comments

Name	Wishes and Comments

Name   Wishes and Comments

Name   Wishes and Comments

Name   Wishes and Comments

Name   Wishes and Comments

Name	Wishes and Comments

Name	Wishes and Comments

Name	Wishes and Comments

Name	Wishes and Comments

Name	Wishes and Comments

Name	Wishes and Comments

Name	Wishes and Comments

Name	Wishes and Comments

Name	Wishes and Comments
Name	Wishes and Comments
Name	Wishes and Comments
Name	Wishes and Comments

Name	Wishes and Comments

Name	Wishes and Comments

Name	Wishes and Comments

Name	Wishes and Comments

Name

Wishes and Comments

Name

Wishes and Comments

Name

Wishes and Comments

Name

Wishes and Comments

Name	Wishes and Comments
Name	Wishes and Comments
Name	Wishes and Comments
Name	Wishes and Comments

Name	Wishes and Comments
Name	Wishes and Comments
Name	Wishes and Comments
Name	Wishes and Comments

Name

Wishes and Comments

Name

Wishes and Comments

Name

Wishes and Comments

Name

Wishes and Comments

Name

Wishes and Comments

Name

Wishes and Comments

Name

Wishes and Comments

Name

Wishes and Comments

Name	Wishes and Comments

Name	Wishes and Comments

Name	Wishes and Comments

Name	Wishes and Comments

Name	Wishes and Comments

Name	Wishes and Comments

Name	Wishes and Comments

Name	Wishes and Comments

Name   Wishes and Comments

Name   Wishes and Comments

Name   Wishes and Comments

Name   Wishes and Comments

Name	Wishes and Comments
Name	Wishes and Comments
Name	Wishes and Comments
Name	Wishes and Comments

Name	Wishes and Comments

Name	Wishes and Comments

Name	Wishes and Comments

Name	Wishes and Comments

Name	Wishes and Comments
Name	Wishes and Comments
Name	Wishes and Comments
Name	Wishes and Comments

Name

Wishes and Comments

Name

Wishes and Comments

Name

Wishes and Comments

Name

Wishes and Comments

Name | Wishes and Comments

Name | Wishes and Comments

Name | Wishes and Comments

Name | Wishes and Comments

Name   Wishes and Comments

Name   Wishes and Comments

Name   Wishes and Comments

Name   Wishes and Comments

Name   *Wishes and Comments*

Name   *Wishes and Comments*

Name   *Wishes and Comments*

Name   *Wishes and Comments*

Name	Wishes and Comments

Name	Wishes and Comments

Name	Wishes and Comments

Name	Wishes and Comments

Name	Wishes and Comments

Name	Wishes and Comments

Name	Wishes and Comments

Name	Wishes and Comments

Name

Wishes and Comments

Name

Wishes and Comments

Name

Wishes and Comments

Name

Wishes and Comments

Name	Wishes and Comments
Name	Wishes and Comments
Name	Wishes and Comments
Name	Wishes and Comments

Name	Wishes and Comments

Name	Wishes and Comments

Name	Wishes and Comments

Name	Wishes and Comments

Name	Wishes and Comments
Name	Wishes and Comments
Name	Wishes and Comments
Name	Wishes and Comments

Name	Wishes and Comments

Name	Wishes and Comments

Name	Wishes and Comments

Name	Wishes and Comments

Name	Wishes and Comments

Name	Wishes and Comments

Name	Wishes and Comments

Name	Wishes and Comments

Name	Wishes and Comments

Name	Wishes and Comments

Name	Wishes and Comments

Name	Wishes and Comments

Name

Wishes and Comments

Name

Wishes and Comments

Name

Wishes and Comments

Name

Wishes and Comments

Name	Wishes and Comments

Name   Wishes and Comments

Name   Wishes and Comments

Name   Wishes and Comments

Name   Wishes and Comments

Name Wishes and Comments

Name Wishes and Comments

Name Wishes and Comments

Name Wishes and Comments

Name   Wishes and Comments

Name   Wishes and Comments

Name   Wishes and Comments

Name   Wishes and Comments

Name	Wishes and Comments

Name	Wishes and Comments

Name	Wishes and Comments

Name	Wishes and Comments

Name

Wishes and Comments

Name

Wishes and Comments

Name

Wishes and Comments

Name

Wishes and Comments

Name

Wishes and Comments

Name

Wishes and Comments

Name

Wishes and Comments

Name

Wishes and Comments

Name	Wishes and Comments
Name	Wishes and Comments
Name	Wishes and Comments
Name	Wishes and Comments

Name

Wishes and Comments

Name

Wishes and Comments

Name

Wishes and Comments

Name

Wishes and Comments

Name

Wishes and Comments

Name

Wishes and Comments

Name

Wishes and Comments

Name

Wishes and Comments

Name

Wishes and Comments

Name

Wishes and Comments

Name

Wishes and Comments

Name

Wishes and Comments

Name

Wishes and Comments

Name

Wishes and Comments

Name

Wishes and Comments

Name

Wishes and Comments

Name	Wishes and Comments

Name	Wishes and Comments

Name	Wishes and Comments

Name	Wishes and Comments

Name

Wishes and Comments

Name

Wishes and Comments

Name

Wishes and Comments

Name

Wishes and Comments

Name

Wishes and Comments

Name

Wishes and Comments

Name

Wishes and Comments

Name

Wishes and Comments

Name   Wishes and Comments

Name   Wishes and Comments

Name   Wishes and Comments

Name   Wishes and Comments

Name

Wishes and Comments

Name

Wishes and Comments

Name

Wishes and Comments

Name

Wishes and Comments

Name   Wishes and Comments

Name   Wishes and Comments

Name   Wishes and Comments

Name   Wishes and Comments

Name	Wishes and Comments

Name	Wishes and Comments

Name	Wishes and Comments

Name	Wishes and Comments

Name	Wishes and Comments
Name	Wishes and Comments
Name	Wishes and Comments
Name	Wishes and Comments

Name   Wishes and Comments

Name   Wishes and Comments

Name   Wishes and Comments

Name   Wishes and Comments

Name   Wishes and Comments

Name   Wishes and Comments

Name   Wishes and Comments

Name   Wishes and Comments

Name   Wishes and Comments

Name   Wishes and Comments

Name   Wishes and Comments

Name   Wishes and Comments

Name | Wishes and Comments

Name | Wishes and Comments

Name | Wishes and Comments

Name | Wishes and Comments

Name   Wishes and Comments

Name   Wishes and Comments

Name   Wishes and Comments

Name   Wishes and Comments

Name

Wishes and Comments

Name

Wishes and Comments

Name

Wishes and Comments

Name

Wishes and Comments

www.ingramcontent.com/pod-product-compliance
Lightning Source LLC
Chambersburg PA
CBHW040835300326
41914CB00061B/1411

9 781839 903274